Charles Jenkinson

A Discourse on the Establishment of a National and Constitutional Force in England

Charles Jenkinson

A Discourse on the Establishment of a National and Constitutional Force in England

ISBN/EAN: 9783337778200

Printed in Europe, USA, Canada, Australia, Japan

Cover: Foto ©Suzi / pixelio.de

More available books at **www.hansebooks.com**

A

DISCOURSE

ON THE

ESTABLISHMENT

OF A

NATIONAL and CONSTITUTIONAL

FORCE

IN

ENGLAND.

BY
CHARLES LORD HAWKESBURY.

LONDON:

PRINTED FOR JOHN STOCKDALE, PICCADILLY,

1794.

[Price Two Shillings and Six-pence..]

ADVERTISEMENT.

THE following Tract was firſt publiſhed in the year one thouſand ſeven hundred and fifty-ſeven, and notwithſtanding it was uſhered into the world without a name, it had the deſired effect. From the general fate of anonymous pamphlets, it has become extremely ſcarce, and of courſe not to be purchaſed at any price. Thoſe who had it in their poſſeſſion knew too well the value of the work to permit it to paſs out of their hands. The publiſher has been induced, by the opinion of ſeveral gentlemen, to think that ſuch a work, at this critical time, may not be unintereſting to the public. It is but juſtice to the writer, that the reader ſhould be informed, the book is re-printed without one word being altered, or the leaſt addition made. The reader will bear in mind, that the dates ſtand as in the work originally publiſhed in 1757.

Piccadilly,
18th February, 1794.

A
DISCOURSE

ON THE

ESTABLISHMENT

OF A

NATIONAL and CONSTITUTIONAL

FORCE

IN

ENGLAND.

THE Conftitution of every free Government is fubject from time to time to a fort
of dangerous Crifis; which demands the attention of all who are concerned for its prefervation; a body, whofe parts are fo various,
and fo nicely framed, is by nature liable to
frequent diforders. The fluctuation of Property, the change of Manners, or difpofition
in the People, and the fhifting of Power from
one

one neighbouring ftate to another, muft vari-
oufly affect it : in abfolute Monarchies, evils
of this kind feldom happen, and are eafily
removed by the interpofition of that Power,
whofe Will is the fimple and fole refource
of fuch a Government; but in the more com-
plicated Machine of a free State greater caution muft be ufed; if the Conftitution is only
through Age impaired, it muft be called back
to its firft principles ; but if fome new emer-
gency has arifen, a new Remedy muft be ap-
plied ; fuch an one, however, is as agreeable to
the nature of the Conftitution, and capable of
being woven into the very fpirit of it ; left
it fhould chance to form an intereft contrary to
it, and in the event prove more fatal than the
diforder.

The Hiftory of this country abounds
with more of thefe critical periods than
any other ; and it is owing to the proper
ufe our anceftors made of them, that our
Government has long been advancing by
various fteps towards perfection : they with-
ftood the repeated attempts both of Papal
Innovation and Regal Oppreffion ; and
though their ftruggles frequently produced
violent fevers in the State ; yet the Confti-

3   tution

tution always came forth in more perfect health, and some new security was obtained for our freedom : and whilst almost every other nation of Europe, who, like us, defended from one free and common stock, long ago became the subjects of arbitrary Power, and resigned their Liberty, this country has always proved a faithful Guardian of that sacred depofit, and has alone improved the Blessing.

Posterity, however, owe a double portion of acknowledgement to those great Statesmen, who directed our affairs at the Revolution, for contributing more at that time than any other to the perfection and security of our Constitution : nothing so much illustrates the wise conduct of these men, as comparing their establishments and regulations, with what was done at the preceding period of the Restoration :—Then we find little more than meer temporary expedients, calculated just to resettle the Exiled Family on the Throne; the Rights of King and People were left unascertained ; and what little was done in favour of Liberty, had no sufficient security for its continuance ; the Wounds, that had been so long bleeding,

were

were fo poorly and fo ineffectually tampered with, that in a few years they opened again, and called for abler hands and more powerful remedies to heal them; fuch was the work of the Revolution.—The wounds were then more deeply probed; the caufes, that produced them, were endeavoured to be removed; lafting (and I hope they will prove perpetual) Ordinances were eftablifhed, which fo juftly fettled the various claims of Power, that almoft feventy years have feen no farther difpute on that head: feveral of the regulations that were made at the Reftoration were then repealed, fome as unconftitutional, others as ineffectual; one Statute; however, whofe purport was inadequate to the ufes for which it was intended, remained without amendment; and by its deficiency rendered that happy fettlement not fully complete;—the Militia Act, which paffed the thirteenth of *Charles* the Second, was in itfelf a vague and ill-concerted fcheme; and the deteftable policy of that, and a fubfequent reign, was to difarm the People; and with the utmoft art and application to render this Plan of a Militia ftill more ufelefs, and if any methods were propofed to make

it

it ferviceable, the Court would never fuffer them to be debated; and fuch Officers as were more zealous than others in exercifing their Companies were reprimanded, as Fomenters of Rebellion :—one could have wifhed therefore that thofe perfons, to whom we were indebted for fo many wife regulations in the year 1688, had planned fome new Militia Law, more capable of execution, and more agreeable to the temper of our Conftitution, than that, the defects of which they could not but have perceived; fuch a work would have completely crowned this almoft perfect Eftablifhment ; Liberty would then have refted fecure, whilft her own Votaries held the fword, which gave her protection : and *Britain*, confiding in her own internal force, would have heard unalarmed of any attempt, which a Foreign Power might threaten againft her.

I pay fo great a refpect to the Patriots of that age, that I would willingly affign fome excufe for this apparent neglect :——They might think, perhaps, that the Nation was not as yet fufficiently calm to venture on putting arms in the hands of the People; the late ftorms had been violent, and were but juft over; and many, who condemned

the

the conduct of the abdicated Prince, ftill re-
tained a ftrange attachment to his perfon—At
that time alfo *France* was juft entered into a
war with all her neighbours; and was likely
to find fo much employment for her troops
on her own frontiers, as not to be able to
fpare any confiderable number to invade this
country : our anceftors, therefore, apprehenfive of fome danger at that time in the attempt,
and not convinced of its immediate neceffity,
might perhaps leave this defect to be reme-
died, and more maturely confidered by their
pofterity, giving them this opportunity of following their example, in framing wife regulations for the improvement of their country, by conftituting fuch a Militia, as would
be fufficient for its defence, but in no refpect dangerous to its conftitution; whenever the nation fhould be in a better temper to receive it, and our fituation in regard to any foreign enemy fhould require
its fervice.

Such is our prefent Condition; never was
a free people more unanimous in their attachment to Government; and whoever of
fufpicious Principles yet remain, think it
either imprudent or unfafhionable to profefs openly their opinions: we entered into

a War

a-War with univerfal Impatience; and ftand
fingly againft a powerful Neighbour, who
alone has frequently baffled the united force
of *Europe*, and whofe numerous and unem-
ployed troops are now ready to take every
Opportunity that may offer to invade our
Country :——To this we can oppofe a powerful Fleet, which will, I hope, be fufficient
to keep the Danger at a Diftance ; and yet,
when we contend for fo great a Stake, any
perfon not liable to be alarmed with unreafonable Apprehenfions, would wifh, that fome
farther fecurity was provided, and that fome
internal Conftitutional Defence was eftablifhed; which might preferve us not only
from the Evil, but from (what in a commercial kingdom efpecially is of no fmall confequence) the frequent terrors of it ;—can we
fufficiently wonder, that a country like this,
diftinguifhed by fuch a variety of bleffings,
and where Commerce has heaped up fuch im-
menfe ftores of wealth, fhould be lefs careful
of its own fecurity, than almoft any other
nation upon earth—lefs even than thofe kingdoms, the miferies of whofe governments
make them hardly worth prefervation ?—
And yet, when we confider the natural ad-
vantages which it enjoys, we fhall find no

Country,

Country, perhaps, more capable of its own
defence; it abounds in natives; and, as an
ifland, is not fubject to any fudden or unexpected attack; it wants no garrifoned
Frontier to delay the approach of an enemy;
a fufficient time muft always be given it to
put any well-concerted plan of defence into
execution: as much, however, as we have
been engaged in wars for thefe laft feventy
years, no fuch plan as this has as yet been
eftablifhed;—fudden, temporary, and even-
tually deftructive expedients have been the
whole of our Minifterial Conduct. We have
juft lived from year to year, and all our Political art has been to deliver ourfelves in the
laft Winter from the difficulties which we
had laid ourfelves under in the preceding;—
To obviate, therefore, the plea or neceffity
of this fluctuating conduct, a plan of National
Defence was propofed in the laft Seffions
of Parliament; experience feemed then to
fhew the neceffity of it; and our fituation
required the immediate ufe of it; we were
at vaft expences, and yet we neither did or
feemed able to do any thing: our Colonies
were unprotected; our Fleets were inactive,
we even trembled for our Mother Country:
the fate of this plan is too well known; it ob-

tained the unanimous confent of the Commons of *Great Britain*, and paffed after various amend-ments and mature deliberations the lower Houfe of Parliament; and juft as it was on the verge of life, was crufhed and rejected in the upper.

I meddle not with the Proceedings of thofe great Affemblies, to whofe decifions I pay a proper deference, though I am unacquainted with their reafons; I fhall only confider thofe argu-ments, which I have heard without doors urged againft this plan by thofe very few, who were not favourers of it.

The firft and principal objection that has been made to this bill is, " that it will abridge " the Prerogative of the Crown, to whom the " Executive Power over the Militia is faid to " have always belonged, by obliging the King, " before he calls it into actual fervice, to com- " municate the occafion thereof firft to Par- " liament."

I am forry by this objection to find a dif-pute again ftarted; which fo much divided the Lawyers and Antiquarians of the laft century, and was one great caufe of all the blood that was fhed in thofe unhappy quarrels; efpecially as the various claims of Power feem to be fairly compromifed by this

Claufe;

Clauſe; the command of the Militia being
given neither to the Crown, nor to the Legiſlature ſeparately; the principal part however, of the execution being lodged in the
King, ſubject in the caſe alone of calling
them out, to one reſtriction from the Parliament: and if the ſentiments of the wiſeſt
men, unſupported by arguments, could ſingly
have any weight on a rational mind, I could
ſafely reſt this point on the opinions of
Mr. *Seldon* and Mr. *Whitlock*, the firſt of
whom ſpoke ſo warmly in the Houſe of Commons againſt the ſole power that was claimed
by *Charles* the Firſt over the Militia, that the
Court imputed to the influence of his arguments more than any thing elſe, the Vote that
was paſſed againſt them on that head; and
the latter as plainly declared in the ſame
place, " that the power of the Militia was
" not, according to Law, ſolely in the Crown,
" but in the King and Parliament jointly;"
and yet theſe men were not looked upon as
over-violent ſpirits in thoſe days: *Charles*
had ſo good an opinion of the former, that
he deſigned the higheſt employment of the
Law in his favour: and whoever peruſes
the ſpeech of the latter, from whence the
above

above fentiment is extracted,* will be ·fuf-
ficiently fatisfied of his moderation.—That
we may not however rely folely on the opinion of others, it may not be amifs to look
a little into what accounts remain of the feveral forts of Militia, that have exifted in
this Country: the fubject is dark and ab-
ftrufe; and yet fome traces may perhaps from
thence be difcovered of the refpective powers,
that have in that particular been lodged
either in King or People; and though our
inquiries on that head fhould not be fuccefsful, they will lead us at leaft to the
knowledge of thofe armies in which our anceftors placed their fafety; and from what
difference of policy it has arifen, that this
kingdom, when neither fo wealthy nor fo
populous as at prefent, had yet a greater internal force within it, and was more fecure
from foreign Invafions.

Our *Saxon* anceftors, as much as they are
ridiculed for their ignorance and barbarity,
were poffeffed of one piece of knowledge,
fuperior in real ufe to many modern refine-
ments, I mean that of wifely conftituting

* See the fpeech in *Rufhworth.*

civil

civil focieties ; their military eftablifhments were, however, the moft diftinguifhing parts of their Governments ; by thefe they were all bound to the defence of their country, whenever it was attacked ; and the nature indeed of fociety feems to require, that they, who enter into it for the prefervation of their property, fhould equally join in repelling any attempt that might be made upon it ; this obligation, therefore, was the common fealty and allegiance which every native owed ; and which, if neglected or refufed, according to the old *Saxon* Law, rendered the party guilty of High Treafon againft his Country, and his eftate under the penalty of forfeiture : —Thefe were called forth into fervice as often as occafion required, by the command of the General Affembly or Gemot ; and fo far was the chief Magiftrate from having any authority in this refpect, that as long as our anceftors remained in *Germany*, he was himfelf occafionally chofen by the fame affembly, that gave orders for this Militia to march ; but when the *Saxons* came over into this ifland, and the office of principal Magiftrate thro' the neceffity of affairs, from temporary became perpetual, the power of the Militia ftill continued

continued in the fame hands; the King indeed
went in and out before his People, and led
them to battle; but he could not legally call
them out into fervice without the common
confent; and though on fome urgent and ex-
traordinary events the ufual forms of government in thofe fimple ages might be omitted,
and the People confiding in their Prince
might come forth at his fole motion to defend
their Country; yet this they did upon confideration of the neceffity, not from any
opinion of the right; once a year they were
conftantly muftered; and when they went to
war, they collected themfelves together in
thofe little bodies, called Decennaries, and
thereby each man fought in the fight of his
Relations or Affociates: their rule of Difcipline was ftrict; it was not however fettled at
the difcretion of the Prince, but by the orders
of the general Gemot.

At length, however, when the Feodal
Tenures came to be grafted on the old *Saxon*
conftitution, another fpecies of Militia was
then in vogue, more acceptable to Princes of an
arbitrary turn of mind than the former, as
being more fubject to their commands; this
may be termed the Feodal Militia, to diftinguifh

C   it

it from the other, which I call the *Saxon* or National.

It is not neceffary to my prefent purpofe to confider how or at what time thefe Tenures firft took their rife; or by what means they came to be fo univerfal ; it is fufficient to fay, that during the reigns of the firft *Norman* Kings they were at their greateft height ; of thefe Tenures, Knights-fervice was the principal ; all who held by this, were fubject by the law of Property to certain military Duties, and were under the command of the Crown, not fo much as King of the Realm, as the great Lord Paramount of the Fee. In the time of the Conqueror they who held by Knights-fervice, were more than fixty thoufand ; for that martial Prince having got the greateſt part of the national property into his hands under the pretence of confifcation, granted it out as a reward to his Barons ; and they again fubdivided it among their followers, fubject always to the obligation of attending their Lords in the Wars. He even obliged the Ecclefiaftical Fees to fubmit to thefe kinds of fervice : this fpecies of Militia is fo generally underftood, that a fhort defcription

defcription of it will be fufficient—When
the King called on his Barons, they attend-
ed, 'and brought under their Banners all
who held any military Fee under them ;
who were by Law obliged to be confiantly
furnifhed with a proper portion of arms ;
thefe were the common foldiers ; and the
officers were certain Retainers, men who
were particularly devoted to the perfon of
their Lords ; who lived in their houfes,
and fubfifled by their bounty : thus every
regiment was a fort of family, of which the
Baron was both Leader and Mafter ; all
were obliged to a fervice of forty days at
their own expence ; and if they continued
longer in the field, the King was to pay
them ; and whenever any one (as being a
minor, or through any other inability) could
not ferve in perfon, the King had poffeffion
of the Fee, and appointed a fubflitute in
his ftead : there were others befides thefe,
who held lands under the obligation of pro-
tecting the borders of the Kingdom towards
Scotland and *Wales*, whenever they were
invaded ; and others who held a Tenure,
called *Caflle-guard*, becaufe they were bound

to the defence of fome particular Fortrefs in cafe of a fiege.

Thus the Crown had got an Army at its difpofal, which it could call out as often, though not for fo long a continuance, as it defired ; and future Princes might hereby have rendered themfelves abfolute, if the firft *William* had not been guilty of one fortunate miftake, by dividing the fhares of Property into too large parcels, making his Barons thereby fo powerful, as to enable them frequently to refufe their fervices both to himfelf and his fucceffors, and by that means to refift their oppreffions.

But the Power of the Crown over this Militia cannot be urged as an argument in favour of the fame claim over any other fpecies ; fince the perfons, of whom this confifted, were bound to thefe duties, not as Subjects, but as Tenants ; not as Freemen, but as Dependants ; not from any principle of the Conftitution, but only by the Law of Tenures ; as Tenants, they were diftrained if they omitted their duty ; and as Tenants, they freed themfelves from any further obligation, by quitting their Fee ; they held their lands by way of payment

for

for what they did; and their poffeffions were termed " Beneficia" Rewards : Militias of this fort are allowed of in the moft abfolute governments ; fuch are at prefent the Zaims and Timariots of the *Turkish* Empire; what inference can, therefore, be drawn from all this, that can in the leaft relate to the prefent queftion, unlefs it be, that the ill ufe which Kings of an arbitrary difpo-fition endeavoured to make of this body of men, too clearly proves, that fuch a power could never yet be entrufted for any fpace of time in thofe hands under any right or pre-tence whatfoever, without fome danger arifing to the conftitution ?

For thefe Tenures (which ought not to be confidered as part of the original frame of our Government, but rather as an evil ex-crefcence from it) proved for a long time a heavy Burden to the Freedom of this Coun-try, and almoft caufed its Deftruction ; to thefe are to be imputed all the arbitrary Acts that were performed by fucceeding Kings for two or three centuries ; under pretence of thefe, illegal Taxes were exacted, and oppreffive courts were erected. The tenure itfelf is however totally now taken away by
                                        ftatute,

ſtatute, and all its ill effects have periſhed with it.

As this new kind of Militia was the favourite of the Crown, the *Saxon* or National lay for ſome time very much neglected: we have, however, ſome diſtant traces of it in the time of *Henry* the Second, and *Henry* the Third, when certain Aſſizes or Aſſeſſments of Arms were made, which determined the particular portion that each man was to have according to his poſſeſſions: but the firſt mention we meet thereof in our Statutes is in the thirteenth year of *Edward* the Firſt, when it was enacted, " That all Natives ſhould be armed " that were between the ages of fifteen " years and forty; they who had fifteen " Pounds a year in land, or forty Marks " in goods, were to keep by them the Arms " of a Horſeman; and they the whole of " whoſe poſſeſſions were inferior to twenty " Marks, were not to be without their " Sword and Battle-ax to defend their " country."—Conſtables were to be choſen twice every year, who in their reſpective Hundreds were to have the inſpection of Arms, and to preſent Defaulters; and we

are

are told at the beginning of this Statute,
that this was no new Law or Inftitution,
but all was done " according to the ancient
" Affize."

But when *Edward* the Second fucceeded
his Father on the Throne, among the many other irregularities of his Government,
he feems to have ufurped a greater power
over this Militia than the Law allowed him ;
for at the re-fettlement of the Government
in the firft year of his Succeffor *Edward*
the Third, the Parliament again declared,
that no one fhould be compelled to arm
himfelf, but as the Cuftom was in former
times ; and the latter part of this Statute
contains fomething neceffary for our obfervation ; for it is there enacted, " that none
" fhall be diftrained to go out of their
" Counties" (I ufe the words of the Statute
roll) " unlefs becaufe of the neceffity of the
" fudden coming of ftrange Enemies in-
" to the Realm :" So that though the Parliament did hereby impower the King to
call out the militia on an urgent occafion ;
yet they fhewed, that they would themfelves be " judges of that occafion," and
that no original Right or Power of that nature was in the Crown, but fuch only as
they

they were pleafed to allow it; and fo cauti-
ous were they in this refpcct, that they
would not let " neceffity in general " ftand
as the Foundation of this Grant, but they
were refolved to explain " this neceffity"
themfelves.—It fhould be only " the com-
" ing of foreign Enemies into the Realm;"
fo that it did not relate " to domeftic
" Troubles or Rebellion ;"—it fhould alfo be
" the fudden coming;" fo that probably
the Invafion muft be actual, before they
could be drawn out of their Counties, and
not the apprehenfion of it only;—it muft
not be of public notoriety, or of which any
preceding Information could be obtained;
for in fuch cafe the ordinary courfe of Parliament muft be taken: and as a proof of
this, we find that two Acts were paffed in
this Reign expreffly for calling out the Militia on two particular occafions; fometimes the Parliament would confine thefe
arrays to the Counties on this fide the *Hum-
ber*; and fometimes to thofe adjoining to the
fea; and fo tenacious were our Anceftors of
all their legal Rights, that we find them again
infifting on this fame Doctrine in the
twenty-fifth year of this Reign, and very
particularly diftinguifhing the difference of

3   autho-

authority, which the Crown could legally ex-
ercife over the Feodal or over the National
Militia.

When this great King was gone to reft,
his Grandfon *Richard* the Second fucceeded
to the Crown, a Prince unlike his Predeceffor
in every Regal Accomplifhment, but much
refembling the fecond *Edward* both in fail-
ings and fate; like him alfo he feems to
have tranfgreffed the bounds the Parliament gave his power over this Militia; fo
that our anceftors found it neceffary again
to re-affert their Rights in this refpect, and
in the fourth year of his Succeffor *Henry*
the Fourth, to re-enact all the preceding
Acts of Parliament that relate to it; and the
Commons Petition, on which this Statute
is grounded, concludes with thefe empha-
tical words, " that all the Commiffions and
" Writs, made contrary to the faid Statutes
" (concerning the Militia), and all the In-
" dictments and Accufations, Obligations
" and Ties made by Colour of the faid
" Commiffions and Writs, with all the De-
" pendings and Circumftances thereto be-
" longing, be cancelled, revoked, quafhed,
" and difannulled for ever, as things made

D   " againft

" againſt Law, and that they may not be
" taken for example in time to come."—
With what free and bold expreſſions does
this Parliament teach us to aſſert our own
Rights, and to take care that, from any timid acquieſcence of ours, no ill conſequence
ſhould ariſe, that may affect the Freedom of
our Poſterity?

I find little to our preſent purpoſe in the
ſeveral following Reigns:—*Henry* the Fifth
was conſtantly engaged in Foreign Conqueſts, and all his ſucceſſors to *Henry* the
Seventh, in civil Contentions, in neither of
which the national Militia could have any
concern; the Annals, therefore, of theſe
times are totally ſilent about it:—Neither
will *Henry* the Seventh, who ſucceeded to
theſe troubleſome days, afford us much
matter on this head; the ancient Laws remained unaltered, though the execution of
them was not greatly, perhaps, regarded.
This King was of too arbitrary a turn of
mind to be fond of national Militia: every
part of the Conſtitution was declining apace,
and *Henry*, and all his deſcendants of the
family of *Tudor*, made too frequent infringe-
ments upon it; troops of this ſort were beginning

ginning now indeed to be unfashionable in *Europe*; *Lewis* the Eleventh had lately established a standing force in *France*; and *Henry*, who had spent his days of exile in that part of the world, had learnt from thence, how unfit a constitutional Militia was for the illegal purposes of Prerogative; he endeavoured therefore to constitute a new species of his own, and having sold variety of Annuities, and granted great numbers of Patents, he got the Parliament twice in his reign to declare, that all his Annuitants and Patentees were obliged, by reason and duty, to attend him to his wars, whensoever or wheresoever he called upon them; and his People seem to have been glad to be quit with him by this concession only, whose arbitrary views, from the wording of the Preambles of these Statutes, appear to have extended much farther; but as it is not probable that these his Pensioners could form any considerable strength, the chief use, which this avaricious Prince made of these Acts, was to fleece his own creatures under pretence of Fines and Compositions: these Statutes, however, continued no longer in force than his Life.

The

The next material particular that concerns the Militia, we meet within the Reign of Queen *Mary*, in the fourth year of which we find that a new affeffment of Arms was made upon the People according to their .Poffeffions ; that, which had been made fo long ago as the thirteenth of *Edward* the Firft, remained ftill in force ; the proportions of it were, however, become very unequal, as Property had fince that time very much increafed in value, and paffed through various alterations. This laft Affeffment purfued the fame plan as the former, and affeffed not only the Poffeffors of Lands, but alfo of Goods, and went fo low, that he, whofe wealth exceeded not the value of Ten Pounds in Chattels, was comprehended in it ; but this Statute, by reafon of the too great proportions which it impofed, lafted not long ; for, in the firft year of *James* the Firft, it was repealed ; and, by the twenty-fifth of the fame King, the thirteenth of *Edward* the Firft was alfo taken away.

So that this Species of a Militia feems by thefe repeals to have been wholly extinguifhed ; and though that great obligation (which every member of fociety muft al-

ways be under, and which was one of the firſt
principles of our Conſtitution), of being obliged
to defend the Community, whenever it was
attacked, could not but ſtill ſubſiſt; yet as no
poſitive Law was left to direct the ſubject in
what manner he was to give his aſſiſtance; the
whole remained in confuſion and uncertainty,
and from hence in part aroſe that variety of
opinions on this head, and thoſe unhappy
Contentions, which we meet with in the ſuc-
ceeding Reign.

When, however, I look back upon the
ſhort account I have been able to collect of
thoſe kinds of Militia, that have been
eſtabliſhed in this country, I cannot help
at the ſame time but acknowledge, that
ſome of the worſt of our Kings did but
very imperfectly conform to the rules that
were preſcribed to them in this reſpect;
and I am conſcious, that ſome Writs or
Commiſſions may, perhaps, be produced to
prove that they ſometimes exerciſed an ab-
ſolute power over the Militia; but theſe, if
they are not founded on ſome law, ſhew
only what they did, not what they ought to
have done; and are proofs not of a Right, but
a Uſurpation. Our Conſtitution was always
free, but the power of the Crown was not
always

always fufficiently circumfcribed; Parliaments did not always fpeak in fo loud a tone as at prefent, and Kings would fometimes fpeak in a louder; and in the intervals of the former they would order out illegal Writs, which can be confidered only as the declarations of the Crown; and that ought not, I am fure, to be judge in its own concern; and as no Statute can be found on which thefe writs can be eftablifhed, we may fairly conclude with the honeft Commons in the reign of *Henry* the Fourth, " that all fuch are null for ever as made againft Law, and ought not to be taken for example in time to come;" the frequent tranfgreffions of Kings againft thefe Militia Laws, obliged our Anceftors, as we have fhewn, fo frequently to re-enact them; this, however, does not impair their credit.—The force of Magna Charta is by no means diminifhed, though repeated Ufurpations obliged the People to infift more than thirty times on its confirmation.

From what has been faid I may be permitted, I hope, to conclude,—that the Conftitutional Defence of this nation has always confifted of its own Natives, drawn into the field, either as their Tenures obliged them,

or

or as the Parliament directed;—and that the people were formerly by law obliged to be armed, fo far were they from having their Arms by Law taken from them—that the Feodal Militia was properly the Army of the King, the National Militia was the Army of the Kingdom; over the firft the power of the Crown was confiderable; over the latter it had originally and abfolutely no power, but fuch only as the Parliament was pleafed to allow it; who, in the cafe of calling that Militia into fervice, were always judges of the occafion;—and laftly, that the National Militia met with encouragement or not, as the reigning monarch was well or ill-intentioned towards his People: the firft and third *Edwards*, (Princes whofe memories will ever be revered, the one as the *Juftinian* of this Country, the other as its moft accomplifhed Warrior) always favoured and encouraged it; while *Edward* the Second and *Richard* the Second (thofe rivals in brutal lufts, folly, and oppreffion,) ufurped upon the Rights of this body, and rendered ineffectual thofe good Statutes, which were paffed for its prefervation.

Permit me alfo here to make one farther obfervation on the care our Anceftors took to keep this country in a state of defence: various Statutes were passed to prevent the exportation of Horses, others for the improvement of the breed, and to oblige persons of property to keep always a certain number by them;—the price also of bows was determinately fixed by Law; the Makers of them were obliged to have never less than fifty made ready in their shops; and the materials of which they were formed were appointed by Parliament as a sort of Toll, without a certain quantity of which no Tun of Merchandise could from some countries be imported into this Kingdom; and as much as our Progenitors are famed for sometimes indulging their genius, a Butt of *Malmsey* could not find its way into their cellars, without a sheaf of arrows for its passport.

I pass now from the history of ancient Militias, to give some account of that which was established in their stead at the Restoration; the Favourers of the undue Prerogative of the Crown in this respect, lay great stress on the Preamble of the Militia Act passed at that time, which says, " that the " power of the Militia is solely and absolutely " in the King, and that neither House of " Parlia-

" Parliament can or ought to pretend to the
" fame, or can lawfully wage any war either
" offenfive or defenfive againft the Crown;"
—and to give the greater weight to this argument, much has been faid of the wifdom
of that Parliament which enacted it, and of
the great characters of the Earls of *Clarendon*
and *Southampton*, who had then the principal di-
rection of affairs:—It will be neceffary therefore to confider the temper both of this
Parliament, and of the perfons who bore
the greateft fway in it, that we may know;
how far we ought to rely on their opinions.

This Parliament, (to which the difgrace-
ful name of Penfionary was given) met firft
in the year 1661, and falfely imputing to
the principle of refiftance the preceding con-
fufions, which were chiefly owing to the
unreafonable paffions and humours of fome
of thofe who refifted, run violently into
the contrary extreme; and by their Laws
did not leave the People a poffibility of
withftanding any arbitrary Encroachments
againft their Privileges, whenever they fhould
have caufe to do it. I need not enter into
a long deduction of facts to prove this:—

E. befides

- befides the above recited Preamble, the
Oaths and Tefts which were then enacted,
are fufficient teftimonies of it; and *Algernon*
Sidney allows the conduct of this Parliament
to be an unhappy proof, that bodies of this
fort may fometimes err; and even at the time
it fat, fome were bold enough to declare,
" that no Conveyancer could in more com-
" pendious Terms have drawn a diffettlement
" of the whole Birthright of England."

In the firft Seffion of this Parliament this
Militia Bill paffed; it was not, however,
without oppofition, as too much favouring
the principle of Non-refiftance; Mr. *Finch*,
the Attorney-General, chiefly promoted it;
it does not appear, that Lord *Clarendon* took
any particular part in it; neither ought the
fentiments of a man, who had acted through
the whole civil wars as a partifan on the
fide of two encroaching monarchs, to be
much regarded in a queftion of prerogative;
it is certain, however, that Lord *Southampton*
objected to fome parts of this Bill; this was
one of thofe things, in which he checked
the over-hafty zeal of that froward Affembly, and fhewed he could be a good fervant
of the Crown without betraying the Rights

of

of the People; he moved himfelf for an amendment in the Militia Oath (which contains the very fame fenfe as the latter part of the Preamble expreffed in terms perhaps lefs exceptionable) as too much encouraging Arbitrary Pretenfions in the Crown; and though Lord *Anglefey* and a majority oppofed this amendment; yet it ferves to fhew, what opinion this noble Patriot entertained of that Teft, and implies alfo what he thought of the Preamble; and even they who fpoke againft this alteration of the Oath, did not prefume to argue againft the Principle upon which it was propofed; but urged, that the Nation would neceffarily underftand the Oath in the fenfe of the Amendment, though the words remained un-altered.

Many years did not pafs before this Houfe of Lords, who had thus rejected the opinion of their illuftrious Member, feemed to repent of their own Act, and paffed another. Militia Bill (which went, alfo through the Lower Houfe) founded on very different principles, and placing the command there-of not in the fame hands as the former, wherein they had paid fo little attention to

E 2   the

the prerogative of the Crown in this refpect, that *Charles* the Second refuſed to paſs it, " becaufe (as he himfelf exprefſed it) he " fhould thereby be deprived of a power, " which he would never confent to part with, " even for half an hour."

We have already obferved that the Affair of the Militia was very much neglected at the Revolution, and have fhewn the reafons of it : the univerfal conduct however of the nation upon that event, fhews clearly, that it was their opinion, that the power of arming the People was not ſo entirely in the Crown, but that they might, as the laſt réſource, take up even offenfive Arms againſt it ; and we are not indeed wholly without a fort of parliamentary Decifion in this particular; for by the firſt of *William* and *Mary* the Oath which declares it " to be illegal " to take up arms againſt any one commif- " fioned by the King," was repealed as un- conftitutional ; and as this Oath contains the fame fenfe as the latter part of the Preamble ; and as the former part of this laſt tends in the event to render any refiſtance to the moſt arbitrary oppreffions impracticable, I fhall leave it to the impartial to determine, how

how far the credit of the whole ought to be affected by this repeal.—The laſt time the neceſſity of a new Militia law was conſidered by the public was juſt after the treaty of *Ryſwick*; when a long foreign war being ended, and the nation reſtored to peace, it was thought a proper opportunity to plan ſuch a ſcheme, and it was moſt ardently wiſhed for by all, who were of a true conſtitutional ſpirit; but the Court, who then foreſaw that a neceſſity would from thence ariſe of diſbanding a greater part of the ſtanding army than was agreeable to it, prevented this wiſe deſign from taking effect; it appears, however, by ſome excellent tracts upon this queſtion, publiſhed at that time, that it was the opinion of the Patriots of that Age, that the ſole power granted to the Crown over the Militia by the 12th of *Charles* the Second, was contrary to the firſt Principles of our Conſtitution, and ought in a new Bill to be veſted in other hands.

Lay, therefore, all theſe arguments together—The Hiſtory of ancient Militias;—The declaration of ſeveral Parliaments before the Reſtoration—The peculiar conjuncture in which the Preamble of this Militia

Act

Act was formed—The temper of the Affembly which enacted it—The opinion of the
Earl of *Southampton*, which has been moft re-
lied on, though not truly reprefented in this
point—And, laft of all, what can be collected of the fentiments of fubfequent Parliaments and wife men fince that period—
And then judge, whether all thefe ought not
to outweigh the fole Preamble of an Act
paffed in a Parliament, which for its fervile
compliances with the Crown has been ftiled
the Penfionary, and whether on fuch a foundation alone the Legiflature of this Kingdom ought to be deprived of a power, which
cannot be lodged in other hands with any
permanent fecurity to the Conftitution?

Reafon, indeed, might alone convince us
of the expediency of what I defend; for as
the perfection of every well-conftituted So-
ciety confifts in the freedom and independence of the Legiflative Body, it is eafy to
conjecture, that fuch a Body could not be
free, and could not be abfolute mafters of
their own determinations, who fhould trans-
fer the Power of the Sword out of their own
hands into thofe of any other, whofe temper
would indeed be too mild to opprefs them,

but

but on whose Mercy they muſt depend for protection.

One farther conſideration has been urged on this occaſion, which can never, however, with propriety be mentioned where the power of the Crown is debated, and that is, the CHARACTER OF THE EXCELLENT PERSON who wears it; — the love of ſuch a Monarch might induce a Loyal People to reſign their Rights, if. he had not too much virtue to accept them; not a wiſh for power has appeared; in any one action of his Reign; his ſubjects could not deſire to be more free than he would have them; he has ſhewn himſelf fully ſatisfied with the lawful Authority of a Britiſh King, whoſe peculiar happineſs it is, that, to do good, his power is without bounds;—to do wrong, he has conſtitutionally no power; ſo that in a political ſenſe he may truly be ſaid, to be bleſſed with the knowledge of Good, without being curſt with that of Evil; whoever, therefore, would put him in a capacity of knowing the latter, is ſo far from being a friend to his Prince, that he is his great Enemy and Seducer; one who would drive him from his ſtate of innocence and per-
ſection,

section, and rob the Crown of its moft diftinguifhing Prerogative; which makes it more fecure and glorious to him that wears it than that of any abfolute monarchy can be.

The fecond objection that has been made to the propofed fcheme was, " that it would " alter the difpofitions of the people of this " Country — check the vein and inclina- " tion they fhew at prefent towards com- " merce and manufactures—and convert a " rich and peaceable nation into a military, " and perhaps feditious people;"—I fhall confider what opinion former precedents and reafon would inftruct us to entertain on this point.

There is fomething in the conftitution of every abfolute monarchy that prevents its making any very confiderable progrefs in Trade; in fuch States the enjoyment of property is too precarious; but I think it undeniable, that the Commerce of *Spain* and *France* arrived at the greateft height, of which the nature of fuch governments is capable, at the fame time that the difpofitions of their people were moft turned to war; and that the military and commercial glories of each Nation were nearly at

their

their meridian together:—when *Spain* produced the beft foldiers in *Europe*, and her aim was Univerfal Empire, her commerce was alfo extenfive; the fame fpirit made her both brave and induftrious, gave Courage to her Armies, and Life to her Manufactures, extended her dominions on the European Continent, and fent her to unknown climes in fearch of new wealth and new poffeffions; —but when the glory of her arms was extinguifhed, her Commerce alfo decayed, and fhe became at once both lazy and unwarlike; from the time of the Pyrenean Treaty, *France* gained the afcendant in power, and at the fame time received, as it were, from her rival an inclination towards trade; the chief paffion of her Natives feemed then to be martial glory, and her armies were more numerous than thofe of any other Nation; and yet, during this conjuncture, for the fpace of about forty years, fhe made her largeft advances in Trade.——I enter not into the reafons of this at prefent; the fact alone is fufficient to prove, that a military fpirit and a commercial difpofition have fometimes met in the fame People.

F   But

But, if we caft our eyes on the annals of
Free States, which are more properly the
nurferies of Commerce; we fhall find the
above truth illuftrated in a ftronger manner;
no Country ever made in a few years fo
great a progrefs in Trade as the United
Provinces; their fhipping was at one time
computed to be more than what belonged
to all the reft of *Europe* put together; and
yet their Wealth and Commerce increafed
in this prodigious manner, while they were
engaged in a war of fifty years continuance
in the heart of their own country; while
moft of their trading towns were Fortreffes,
garrifoned by Burghers, and while the natives
of this Republic, from eighteen years of age
to fixty, were obliged by the Union of *Utrecht*,
to be armed and trained; but fince this firft
eftablifhed Militia has been neglected; fince
they trufted their defence to Foreign Mercenaries; and fince of late they have hardly been
defended at all; their Commerce has been gradually on the decline. Sir *William Temple* ob-
ferves, that in his time it was paft its meridian;
and fome approaching period perhaps may fhew
both this and their power fetting together.

Whoever

Whoever alfo has but curforily perufed the
Hiftory of our own Country muft have obferved, that thofe reigns, in which the martial
fpirit of our People has moft appeared,
have been no lefs diftinguifhed by the advances, that were then made in Commerce ;—
I fhall inftance only in the reign of *Edward* the
the Third, when *Scotland*, *France*, and *Spain*,
felt the fuccefsful efforts of our Arms; when
the National Militia was in vogue, often
trained, and frequently called into fervice;
when the Legiflature thought it an object
worthy their attention, and paffed feveral
laws in its favour,—and what part of our
annals can produce more good Statutes in
fupport of trade ? Or, did Commerce at any
time take larger ftrides towards perfection ?—
This cannot be better proved, than by ob-
ferving, that in the twenty-eighth year of this
King, our Exports were to our Imports, as
more than Seven to One; this was a furprifing Balance of Trade in our favour ; and
fhews that our Manufactures muft at that
time have been in a flourifhing condition,
that our people were by no means idle, and
that their Military Accomplifhments, which
they were ready at all times to exert in the

fervice

fervice of the public, proved no obftruction to the attention they otherwife paid to their domeftic occupations.

But we need not enter into a long deduction of hiftorical facts to prove this; fince Reafon, a better guide, will teach us, that a certain degree of Military ftrength in a nation is abfolutely neceffary, as well for the Encouragement as the Prefervation of Trade. Commerce loves fecurity, not fuch as can arife from the protection of another, but fuch as places the power in her own hands; and on which fhe can fully depend.——No one will labour to "have," if he is not certain he fhall be able to "hold."——A precarious poffeffion would be but a bad encouragement to dangerous voyages and painful occupations; and no Merchant will with zeal and pleafure apply himfelf to Trade, unlefs he has a good opinion of the wifdom and conduct of the ftate, that is to fecure his acquifitions; — that it is eftablifhed on foundations which cannot eafily be fhaken, nor confequently in danger of any fudden Revolution; and as he requires good Laws to protect him from domeftic oppreffions, fo muft he no

lefs

lefs have a well-conftituted internal force to
fecure him from foreign invafions.

Befides, we may allow fome degree of
reafonable ambition to every honeft Trader;
which ftimulates him in his profeffion, by
the hopes he entertains of being qualified,
by means of his acquifitions, to bear a fhare
one time or other in the government of his
Country; but if fuch a State is defpicable
abroad, and defencelefs at home, how much
muft this laudable fting and encouragement
be diminifhed, when the Government, by
its ill conduct, is got below his ambition,
and when, long before the happy period of
his pre-eminence can arrive, his Country
and his own poffeffions may have perifhed
together?

And if an internal Force was ever neceffary for the fupport of Trade, it is now
more particularly fo, when our numerous
and diftant Colonies demand the protection
of our Navies—when our Commerce is vul-
nerable in more parts than it was formerly,
and our Fleets muft leave the head of our
dominion, whofe defence was once their
only occupation, to repel every attack that
may be made on the exterior parts of
it;

it ;—they can no longer parade it in our
channel alone ; the moſt diſtant coaſts of
the world demand their ſervice ; and experience convinces us of the neceſſity of
this dilemma, either that we muſt eſtabliſh
an internal Conſtitutional Force for the Defence of our own Country, and ſend forth
our Fleets for the Protection of our Colonies,
or keep our Navy at home for the preſervation
of the former, and leave the latter an eaſy
prey to the firſt enemy that ſhall ſeize upon
them.

Allow, however, for once, the objection
its full force,——" that ſuch an inſtitution
" would check the commercial diſpoſition
" of our people."——But would it in ſuch
a caſe be wiſe to riſk the enjoyment of a
ſufficiency with ſafety, for the ſake of ſome
trifling acquiſition ? Shall we give up our ſe-
curity, which was the principal motive of
our entering into ſociety, for the intereſt of
our Commerce, which is only the embelliſh-
ment of it ? Was not the deſign of Riches
and Trade, to enable a community the better to preſerve its independence ? And ſhall
we, therefore, cultivate the means to that
extravagant degree, as abſolutely to deſtroy

3   the

the end, for which they were eftablifhed;- if we leave our Country defencelefs, the more rich it grows, it becomes the more defireable morfel, and tempts, as it were, its enemies to deftroy it ; Hufbandmen and Artificers muft turn Soldiers, when the conteft is, who fhall have the land and merchandife ; and though *Plato* and *Arif-totle* have juftly blamed *Lycurgus* for having inftilled too martial a fpirit into the. Laws of his Republic ; yet they would certainly have paffed no lefs a cenfure on that Lawgiver, who fhould frame the wifeft inftitutions to make a People free and wealthy, without eftablifhing a proper force for the fecurity of thofe Enjoyments.

But this objection farther urges, " that, " if fuch an Inftitution was neceffary againft " foreign Invafions ; yet by arming the Peo- " ple, they will be made feditious, and " of courfe become dangerous to the inter- " nal frame of the Government."—I fee plainly from whence this apprehenfion firft arofe ;—-Perfons, who perufe the hiftory of this Country, but who from an ignorance of its Laws enter not fufficiently into the fpirit of its Inftitutions, have built this

objection

objection on the civil diffensions which the
Barons were once able to raife by means of
the Feodal Militia; but it is certain that
the People were not as principals concerned
in thofe Wars: not they, but the Barons
were feditious; they fought indeed for their
refpective Lords whenever they called upon
them; but it was not from any fpirit of
Rebellion: it was, becaufe the Law of Tenures commanded, and the neceffity of
fubfiftence obliged them; they were fometimes indeed in a moft unhappy Dilemma,
when the Law of the Crown called them
one way, and the obligation of their Fees
another; this inconvenience, however, ought
not to be confidered as the ill effect of a
Militia; but becaufe the command of it
was lodged in improper hands: this I allow
to be a point of moft ferious confequence.—
As fuch, I have treated it in the former
part of this Difcourfe,—In the propofed Plan
the command is given to thofe, who can
never ufe it to the deftruction of their
Country; over this Militia no undue or
dangerous influence can ever be gained; the
parts, of which it confifts, will be perpetu-
ally changing; it is abfurd therefore to argue
againft

againſt a thing in general, becauſe a particular ſpecies of it has, through a defect in
the inſtitution, been converted to illegal pur-
poſes ; the moſt ſacred things have ſometimes been abuſed ; and it would be childiſh
to impute to any inſtrument the ill effects
that may be produced by it, when a madman
has got it into his poſſeſſion.

. Look through the Annals of the World,
and ſee if any one inſtance of a Militia can
be produced, that was ſeditious of itſelf, or
of a People, who, when the ſword was put
into their hands, converted it to their own
deſtruction. — Free States have almoſt always been ſubject to commotions, and the
ſame have generally been defended by a
Militia ; but that the Military Eſtabliſhments of ſuch a People were the cauſe of
their commotions can never be proved ;—
the Republic of *Carthage* is a ſingular inſtance of a free people, that owed their defence to mercenary ſoldiers ; and yet ſhe
was neverthelcſs fertile in diſſenſions ;—and
though *Rome* had as many Soldiers as Citizens, though her Senators and Plebeians
had frequent conteſts for power, where the
Balance was unequally adjuſted, yet her

G   People,

People, when in the greateft fury, and when driven by injuftice almoft to defpair, never once had recourfe to arms; they urged their claims by fupplications and feceffions; and though difciplined and ready at all times to take up arms in the defence of their Country, they never lifted up a hand againft it; for feveral centuries not a life was loft amidft all their Contentions; and it was not until the nature of their armies was changed, until their legions received pay, were tranfported into diftant Provinces, and never fuffered to return to their domeftic Occupations; in a word, not until the honeft Militia-Men of *Rome* were changed into Standing Forces, that their contefts blazed out into civil wars deftructive to the Commonwealth.

The Miferies and Oppreffions, which fome States have fuffered from the common fort of armies, have made many abfurdly apprehenfive, that a Firelock or a red Coat muft neceffarily alter the difpofition of the perfons who have them; they do not obferve, that thefe evils have arifen from fuch only, who have made war their profeffion; it is the idle and diffolute manner ncr of living, that alone debauches the Soldier's inclination, when without home, without induftry, and without occupation he muft fubfift either by pay or by plunder; Armies compofed of fuch as thefe have fometimes enflaved a Nation under pretence of doing themfelves juftice; our Hiftory furnifhes a remarkable inftance of this kind, which fhews clearly what it is that converts a Soldier into a Rebel, and makes him dangerous to his Country. As gallant an army as this Nation ever faw, and which at the fame time was particularly ftiled the *Modeft* and *Self-denying*, confifted of the Youths of *London*, who, though unufed to arms and drawn in hafte out of Town, gave fignal proof of Courage through the whole Civil Wars, and at laft defeated the Royal Army by one decifive blow at *Nafeby:* If this Army of the Parliament, after they had done the bufinefs for which they were called out, had been fent back to their Trades, and had only been made ufe of, as there was occafion for them, they would then have been in the nature of a Militia, and there would have been no

G 2   danger

danger to have apprehended from them—
but by keeping them for feveral years conftantly in the field, after the war was over,
by training them to idlenefs, and making
them forget their Trades, and depriving
them of the common methods of fubfiftence, they were made not at all the better Soldiers, but became the worfe Citizens ; their difpofitions were totally per-
verted; their modefty changed to prefumption ; they grew imperious and feditious ;
they refufed to go to *Ireland*, though they
were commanded ; neither would they be
difbanded, though the Parliament had no
other occafion for their fervice,—they petiti-
oned — they remonftrated — they rebelled
—and at length deftroyed the Authority of
that Parliament which at firft called them
forth, and had performed fuch wonders by
their affiftance.

I fhall here, therefore, reft this point, and
will only obferve, that whatever force there
is in this laft Objection, it muft hold uni-
verfally againft every fpecies of Militia ; for
if the people by being armed will be made
idle and feditious (and without arming
them

them to fome degree, no Militia, I am fure, can be eftablifhed) it will be a reafon againft every other Plan that fhall be offered ; and they who urge it, muft be againft the principle of a Militia itfelf, or they do not fully comprehend the force of their own arguments ; and when they accufe thofe as guilty of calumny, who on this account affert, that they are againft that Conftitutional Principle, they fhould confider whether they are not themfelves in fact the calumniators, and whether their own words do not convict them of the reproach, which they fo much dread from the tongues of others.

The next Objection that I have heard urged againft a Conftitutional Force of this fort is, " That it is not practicable in this " country ;" let any one reflect that almoft all the ancient Governments, and even this Kingdom, was once defended by a Militia ; let him alfo obferve, that fome nations owe at prefent their protection to it ; and he will need no other argument to convince him, that *England* cannot be fo peculiarly unfortunate, as to be alone incapable

capable of fuch an inftitution ; Abfolute Monarchies would be glad of fuch a defence ;
but they feldom have it, becaufe they dare
not truft it ; the freedom however of this
nation particularly fits it for a Militia ; and
fhall we then reject an advantage, which
the nature of our Government has given us
over moft of the other ftates of *Europe* ?
But it will be faid, perhaps, that it is only
meant, " that the prefent Plan is *impracti-*
" *cable*"—Let a better then be propofed.
——I argue not fo much for particular
fchemes as for general Principles ;—or let
them affign fome reafons for this objection ;
I never heard but one, which was, " *that*
" *the gentlemen of the country would not at-*
" *tend to the execution of it :*" I own, I have
a better opinion of my countrymen ; and I
am fure, the Impatience they have fhewn
for fuch an eftablifhment is a confiderable
prefumption in their favour ; and if they
fhould at length difappoint our expecta-
tions, they will fhew themfelves unworthy
our conftitution, and difqualified for a ftate
of liberty ; and having thus failed in a point
fo indifpenfably neceffary for the fecurity
of

of a free Government, we had better openly at once refign it ;—but if they fhould in fome few particulars neglect their duty, the propofed Scheme has provided an adjutant and forty ferjeants to each battalion ; who are to be conftantly paid and employed in training the men that are under them ; thefe will probably be found alone fufficient for that purpofe ; and are not many lefs, perhaps, than contribute in reality to the difcipline of any one battalion in our fervice ; and as to the fpirit of thefe ruftic officers, when called into the field, I cannot think that the love of liberty, and the love of their country, are yet become fuch antiquated notions, and are fo entirely foreign to their breafts, that they will not animate their conduct in the fame manner, as they once did the conduct of their anceftors ; and that they will not, on a proper occafion, awake in them that public-fpirited enthufiafm which inflames the mind, and kindles a glow of courage within it, fuperior to what the weaker motives of intereft, or even of honour, are able to infpire ; in this refpect, however, our national

character

character would at least make us hope, what nothing but future experience can positively determine.

I allow, indeed, that the talents and knowledge which are requisite to form a great General, must be as extensive as any of which the human mind is capable—but I cannot think that the profession of a common soldier requires either much genius or application; the rest will easily be acquired, if courage be not wanting; and as nature has endowed mankind with different degrees of it, so nothing contributes more to improve and inflame it, than the hope of rewards and the fear of punishments;—the first of these motives will peculiarly affect the militia-man; the preservation of whose freedom, whose freehold, and whose family, will be the consequence and reward of his victories; and if he should not discharge his duty in the time of action, he will be liable equally with the common soldier to all that the Military Law can inflict; and he will suffer the additional punishment of the loss of all his possessions; for if the public enemy should not happen to seize upon them, the enjoy-

ment

ment will still be lost to him, who must quit them through shame, or live on them with dishonour.

If they, who hold the force of such an establishment in contempt, would but peruse the history of their own country, they would find that the *British* Militia was always famous for a truly martial spirit;—in the battles, where this alone was engaged, a much greater number lost their lives, than what are slain in the less bloody encounters of the present age, though the engines of war were then by no means so destructive as at present;—can greater discipline be shewn, than when each man perishes in his rank? And can we doubt the courage of those armies, whose victories were generally so complete, that one alone would often prove conclusive in favour of him who obtained it? Is it that the spirit of our people is decayed? or are the exercises and evolutions of modern armies more difficult than the ancient? or is more genius now required to pull a trigger than formerly to draw a bow-string? Can we no where at present find that steady persevering spirit,

H   which

which fo much diftinguifhed the *London*
Militia at the battle of *Newbury?* And
where is now that glowing courage, which
enabled fifteen hundred men of *Inifkilling*,
almoft without arms, to defeat ten thoufand regular troops entrenched in a bog,
and take their General prifoner?—I may be
thought, perhaps, to degrade the military
art, when I fay, that I can fee no reafon
why a country-fellow may not as cafily learn
to handle his arms as to play at cricket;
and why, like this, it may not become his
diverfion; the public games of ancient governments confifted principally of martial
entertainments; and why may not the *Britifh* Youth amufe themfelves in playing at
foldiers, as well as the *Grecian*, the *Ro-
man?*

All the heroic acts, with which the hif-
tories of thofe Commonwealths abound,
were performed by Militias; they did not
find it impoffible to difcipline their own
citizens; and yet, if we may believe the
modern writers on the art of war, the Tac-
tics of thofe ftates had more of genius,
and were more refined than the prefent;—

moft

moft of the nations alſo of *Europe* were
till within thefe three centuries 'defended
by Militias;—and did not *Holland*, when
her own citizens were obliged to be trained, defend herſelf againſt the power of
Spain? Could the arms of *Philip*, con-
ducted by *the genius* of the Prince of *Parma*,
ever penetrate far into *her* country? and
did not the fieges of *Harlaem*, *Alcamar*, and
Leyden, when they were garriſoned only by
their own Burghers, break the Spirit of
the *Spanifh* veterans? and yet this very
country was over-run, and moft of her
towns taken, in the fpace of a month, in the
year 1672, when the defence thereof was en-
truſted to 25,000 mercenaries:—It is uſeleſs
to cite any more examples;—the very origin
of ftanding forces fhews, that they were not
thought indifpenſably neceſſary for the defence
of a country; they were firſt raiſed to fup-
preſs rebellious ſubjects, to command the un-
willing fubjection of diſtant and oppreſſed
provinces—or to extend the conqueſts of ſome
afpiring Prince into diſtant countries, for
which he could not legally command the fervice of the Militia.

I fhall

I shall leave it to persons who are skilled in military knowledge, to determine, whether the precise number of days that are appointed by this Plan for the training this Body of Men, is sufficient;—if they are not, I am sure they ought to be augmented; and the confideration of some trifling expence, or some little loss in trade, ought not to be put in the balance against Security. The rotation, however, that is propofed, seems to be so far from being an Objection, that Marshal *Saxe*, in his Reveries, has deferibed a method fomething like this, as the best way of recruiting the *French* army; he recommends that the whole People of *France* should be obliged to ferve for five years by turns; this he thinks would be the most probable means of procuring good foldiers; neither does he imply the least doubt from the short time which each individual would in fuch a cafe ferve, that there would be any defect in the difcipline of fuch an army. But I am still more inclined to think, that the Regulations of the propofed Plan are fully adequate to the purpofes for which they

are

are intended; as they exactly correspond
with the rules of the beſt-regulated Militia,
that at preſent ſubſiſts in *Europe*. The regulations of *Switzerland*, and the propoſed
Plan, agree in forming the Militia of Part
only of the people, and recruiting it out of
the remainder.

Both allow Pay in the Time alone of
Service, with this only difference, that the
Swiſs give their Officers double Pay for the
firſt month, to enable them to purchaſe
their Field-Equipages ; and this amendment might not be improperly adopted into
our Plan—Both agree in cloathing their
Militias in a Uniform—in providing a public Depoſitory for their arms—in exerciſing
them after divine Service on *Sundays*—and
in teaching them to hit a mark by ſhooting
at Butts.

The *Swiſs* have an Officer called a Com-
miſſioner of Arms ; whoſe employment is
much the ſame as that of the Adjutant in
our Plan ;—both are to ride from one Company to another, to ſee that the Men are
properly trained, and that they take proper
care of their Arms and Accoutrements ;—
the *Swiſs* have a ſuperior Officer, called a

L   Grand

Grand Major, over every District, whose employment resembles that of the Lord-Lieu-
tenants of our Counties; both command the
Militia of their respective Divisions—are
obliged at certain times to review them—
and to see that all inferior officers discharge
their duty.

Upon the whole, the two Plans differ
only in a few particulars, in which the *English*
one seems to have the advantage.

Four Serjeants are to be appointed to each
Company of the *English* Militia, and are to
be veteran Soldiers draughted out of the regular Corps; these are to be constantly paid,
that they may the better attend to the training of the common men;—nothing of this
sort can be found among the *Swiss* regulations.

The *Swiss* find their own arms, the *English* are to be supplied by the Public; the
latter will probably by this means be better
and more uniformly armed.—The *Swiss*
have several regulations for giving a sudden
alarm in case of an unexpected Invasion,
and for calling their Militia on any emer-
gency together; but our happy Situation,
as an Island, renders all care of this sort
unnecessary,

unneceffary, and puts it out of the power of an Enemy to make any confiderable attempt upon us, without our having notice fufficient to be prepared for it.

It is by means of fuch an Inftitution as this, that the little country of *Switzerland* is able to call together fourfcore thoufand brave men at all times for its defence; and fo fmall is the charge of maintaining them, that although the People of this Republic are lefs loaded with Taxes than thofe of any part of the world befide, yet they are able to fave out of their common Revenue a confiderable fum of money yearly, which they keep in their Treafuries againft any emergent occafion; and the furprifing acts of valour, which this Militia has performed, have induced an ingenious Writer to draw a parallel between the military Achievements of this little Collection of Cantons, and thofe of the free States of *Greece* :—He puts in competition with the Battle of *Marathon*, that of *Morgarten*, where 1300 *Swifs* routed the Army of the Arch-Duke *Leopold*, confifting of 20,000 men, and killed twice their own number :—He confiders the Action of *Sempach*, where the fame Arch-
Duke

Duke loft his life, and 20,000 of his men, were routed by 1600 *Swifs*, as a more furprifing Victory than that of *Platea*;—and, to crown all, the Battle that was fought in the Pafs of *Wefen*, in the Canton of *Glaris*, is a Copy that exceeds its Original .which was fought at *Thermopylæ* : for as 300 *Spartans* tried to repel the army of *Perfia* in thofe Streights, and all perifhed in the attempt ; fo in fuch another. Defile, 350 *Swifs* attacked at leaft 8000 *Auftrians*, and gained the Field of Battle.—It is furprifing, fays this Author, what a Spirit the remembrance of this Action inftils into this People ; they yearly celebrate it by a public Proceffion on the Spot where it was fought ; and where eleven Pillars, erected for that purpofe, fhew the Places where thefe Heroes eleven times rallied ; at each Pillar they offer up Thanks to God, and when they come to the laft, one of their beft Orators makes a Panegyric in Praife of thefe three hundred and fifty men, and at the end of his Oration reads a Lift of their Names in the fame manner as the *Spartans* had the Names of thofe who fell at *Thermopylæ*, carved on Brafs, to tranfmit their Fame to Pofterity.

Shall

Shall we after this therefore laugh at a Militia ?—call it an undifciplined Mob ?——And think it ufelefs for the defence of our Country ?—I wifh only that they, who are guilty of this ridicule, may on the like occafions behave no worfe than thefe *Swifs* ;—or, becaufe arbitrary Princes have for thefe three laft centuries neglected their Militias, and for their own views rendered them purpofely ufelefs and undifciplined, fhall we therefore conclude, that no regulations can bring them back to their ancient perfection, or make them again ferviceable ?—Or fhall we more abfurdly argue, that the fame rules that make a Militia regular and well-difciplined in *Switzerland*, will be unfuccefsful in *England*, and that the fame caufes will not produce the fame effects in one Country as well as another ?

" But it may further, perhaps, be urged, " that a Militia is unneceflary, fince we " may be better defended by augmenting " our National Army, or by hiring foreign " troops."—I fhall anfwer plainly to this objection, that both thefe methods are dangerous and unconfiitutional. — I entertain not thofe abfurd apprehenfions of a

I   ftanding

ftanding Army, that poffefs fome People, neither do I think that 20,000 foldiers of that fort could ever be deftructive to our Conftitution ; but I am confident, that an Army may be fo far augmented as to become deftructive :—I entertain alfo the higheft opinion of the Officers of our prefent Army ; I believe them to have as warm a regard for their Country as any Native whatfoever ; many of them are men of Property, others are heirs or allied to families of Property, and would lofe as much in the general wreck as any : but I am fure, that thefe gentlemen will agree with me, that in fome future century it might be poffible to alter and model fuch an army, and make it confift of Perfons not fo public-fpirited as themfelves ; and if its numbers fhould happen at that time to be confiderably augmented, no more, perhaps, than what would be abfolutely neceffary for our fecurity againft a Foreign Invader, I fhould then (if I chanced to live in fuch an age) be ferioufly apprehenfive indeed for the liberties of my country ;——fo that we are in this Dilemma, either fo keep our Army fo low as to be inadequate to the purpofes

for

for which it is intended,—or to raife it fo
high as to make it one time or other dangerous to our Conftitution; for certain it
is, that any number of Troops which will
be fufficient to repel the ftrength of *France*,
will have the Power, if they fhould have
the Inclination, to enflave us; and that they
who can defeat them, who would otherwife be fuperior to us, muft neceffarily have
this country at their mercy.——Or, if it
was poffible to fuppofe, that an Army, thus
modelled and powerful, could not be induced to defeat, by one hafiy blow, the
public-fpirited labours of fo many Centuries,
and that it would be even wife in a free
People, to rely on their virtue in this particular—may we not fiill have reafon to
apprehend, that by the influence and de-
pendance of fo large a body, an intereft
may be created, dangerous and repugnant to
the fpirit of our Government,—which may
direct the Legiflature in an improper manner,
though it may not at once fubvert it;—which
will operate infenfibly to our deftruction;
and, though lefs violent in its progrefs than
the former Evil, will be no lefs fatal to the
Conftitution ?

Here,

Here, indeed, it may juſtly be replied, that theſe dangers are very far remote, and that we are not only ſecure at preſent from any apprehenſions of this kind, but that we alſo poſſeſs a large ſtock of freedom in reverſion; ſince there is an Heir to the Crown, whom nature has adorned with virtues, peculiarly calculated to make the people of this Country hereafter happy, and who will prolong for many years the free ſpirit of his Grandfather's Government :—But it is the duty of an *Engliſhman* to be even timidly ſuſpicious in the concerns of his liberty, and to labour for its continuance in his moſt remote poſterity ; to accept, with gratitude, the favours of good Princes, but to ſecure himſelf with caution againſt the oppreſſions of the bad.——And, ſhall we not be carelefs Guardians of our Country's Rights, if lulled aſleep by ſome temporary advantage, we ſhould not deſcry a diſtant danger, or through indolence ſhould not labour to prevent it ?

But, if there was no danger in this method, the expence of it is alone a ſufficient reaſon to reject it : a Militia, conſiſting of upwards of 60,000 men, will coſt, one year with another,

under

under 160,000l. and will put the Nation
to no further charge, but only during the time
of an actual invasion :—A regular standing
Force, of the same number, will exceed two
millions a year—8000 *Heffians*, with all the
concomitant expences, for this summer's service only, will cost near 800,000l, and the
whole of the expence of the land forces
for this year, (though we shall have acted
every where on the defensive,) will probably
exceed three millions; and though the establishment of this year will not be equal
to the number proposed by a Militia by several thousands, it will surpass it in expence
by almost twenty times the sum;—I calculate
only in the gross, for my argument does
not require exactness; since the experience
of last winter, and the difficulties which
our Ministers found to discover new Taxes,
on which to borrow the money, plainly proves,
that we shall not long be able, in the time
of war alone, to raise a much less sum
than these calculations require; and we ought
to be at the same expence to keep up these
troops in the time of peace, if we mean
to have them always ready, and to be totally freed from all apprehensions; the most
ignorant,

ignorant, however, muſt know, that a con-
ſtant charge of this fort is beyond the abi-
lities of this exhauſted Country. This alone
would be ſufficient for its deſtruction, and
would ſave its enemies the trouble of an invaſion,

But let us ſuppoſe, " that there would be no
" need of maintaining theſe troops but in
" time of war, and that they might be
" raiſed juſt as occaſion requires."——But
would they, for that reaſon, be the leſs dangerous to our Conſtitution? Is it not at the
evening of a war that thoſe fatal ſtrokes
are generally given, when an Army fluſhed
with its victories, and proud of its achievements, thinks its own merits never ſuffi-
ciently rewarded, and dreads its approaching
diſſolution?——And, is the charge of new
levies ſo very inconſiderable? Which *Mon-
ticuculi* (who underſtood the detail of theſe
things better than any man) obſerved to be
ſo great, that he adviſed his maſter on the
principle of œconomy, to keep the ſame
number of forces always on foot, rather
than be at the expence of raiſing them
afreſh at the commencement of every war;
and would it not in ſuch a ſituation be in
the power of our enemies, by a pretended

I   alarm,

alarm, to force us into such an expence, whenever they pleafed; and almoft to terrify us into our deftruction, and to make us, like fome timid animal, run ourfelves down with fright, when perhaps no real danger is near us?——And after all, can we efteem thefe new levies, raifed in hafte and collected out of the dregs of the people, preferable to, or better difciplined than a National Militia, who will at leaft have learned fomething of their bufinefs before they are called into fervice? I fear, indeed, that it is the inexperience of thefe new levies, that makes *England* feldom fuccefsful at the beginning of a war; and that it is the great expence which they coft, and the great burden, which a Minifter muft necef-farily lie under on fuch an occafion, that makes him never enter into a War fo foon as the intereft of his Country requires.

What a wretched fluttering thing is a *Britifh* Minifter at the eve of a War? More afraid of his private enemies than thofe of his Country; he delays engaging with the one, that he may avoid the attack of the other; and that he may keep his own power the longer unmolefted, he lets the power of his Country be diminifhed, and her honour be infulted — at length, when

the

the enemy have had time to carry their
point, and have already got poffeffion of
what is contended for, compelled by cla-
mour, he plunges into a war :—Confounded
and irrefolute, he now pretends to guide the
Helm of a great State through the ftorm,
with hardly his own wits about him—his
firft ftudy and expence is to protect the
Continent — his fecond to preferve himfelf,
—his laft to defend his country—he is at a
vaft charge for new levies, which will be
raifed, when they are no longer wanted ;
and difciplined by that time they are to
be broken;—and under the pretence of a
neceffity of his own creation he detains the
Britifh Fleet in port, after having expend-
ed millions in equipping it with cannon that
are never to fire, and fails, that are never to be
unfurled.—Is this the art of government? This
fenfelefs, deftructive, ill-concerted piece of con-
fufion? And fhall we prefer this to a Conftitutional Internal Force, on which a regular
plan of action may be formed, which will make
us always fecure at home, and enable us to be
victorious abroad?

One more method of defence remains to
be confidered, which is that in which we

at

at prefent place our truft, "the defence of "foreign Mercenaries." The expence of thefe would alone be a fufficient objection to them, which is greater in every particular, than the charge of a ftanding army of native foldiers; for befides their fub- fiftence, which they receive at the fame rate as our National Troops, we pay for them fubfidy-mony, — levy-money, — tranf- porting-money, — recruiting-money;——every one of which Articles are carried to a vaft height; and for fome of them we pay double what they coft the Prince who fupplies them;—but the more material arguments againft them is, that they are more dangerous even than a ftanding army can be to our Conftitution.—I fhall here fpeak with caution; for if I was to urge all the objections which might be brought againft troops of this fort, efpecially at a time when we are under the unhappy ne- ceffity of employing them, I may appear, perhaps (what I am fure is not my inten- tion) defirous of inflaming; my country- men may form fome idea of their danger from one or two inftances in their own hiftory—troops of this fort have always been unufeful or dangerous to whoever em-

K   ploys

ploys them; their conduct at firſt has generally been peaceable and enſnaring—at
laſt ſeditious and deſtructive; and thoſe
ſtates, that have carried the points, which
they intended by their affiſtance, have
uſually, in the event, been enſlaved by them;
Machiavelli ſpeaks fully on this point, " le
" Mercenarie, ſono inutili & pericoloſe,
" & ſe uno huomo tiene lo ſtato ſuo fon-
" dato in ſu l'armi Mercenarie non farà
" mai fermo ne ſicuro," and afterwards he
affigns the reaſon, " la cagione di queſto,
" ,e, che non hanno altro amore ne altra
" cagione le tenga in campo, che un poco
" di ſtipendio, ilquale non è ſufficiente a
" fare, che ci voglino morire pe te." And
after having produced a great number of
examples out of the hiſtory of the *Italian*
ſtates to prove this, he concludes " & fu
" ſempre opinione & ſententia digli huo-
" mini ſavii, che niente ſia coſi infermo &
" inſtabile, comé la fama della potenza non
" fondata nelle ſerze proprie." There is
alſo a farther reaſon, which *Machiavelli* was
not aware of, that particularly diſqualifies
a free people for any army of this nature;
—the unreaſonable jealouſies which ſuch a
Nation will contract concerning them, and

2   the

the ill-treatment they will in confequence thereof, perhaps, fhew to them, may provoke the moft regular and beft difciplined troops to do that through refentment, which through inclination they never intended; never furely did troops behave themfelves with more exact difcipline than thofe which our Legiflature has thought proper to invite at prefent to our affifiance ; and yet I would afk the good-natured part of my Countrymen, whether, on this occafion, their own ardent and laudable love of liberty, through a miftake in the application of it, has not trefpaffed a little on their humanity ? —And if all the above arguments were infufficient ; it is certainly beneath the dignity of a great and independent Nation to rely upon thofe for its defence, whom they are not fure they can always obtain, when they want them,—or even keep, when their fervice is moft required.

It remains, therefore, that a National Militia is the only defence on which this country can fafely rely, or which it can afford to keep ; the conftant charge of this will be immaterial, and then we fhall only be obliged to part with any confiderable fum for its fupport, when the fafety of the Whole is

K 2   in

in danger ; and if we at the fame time keep
up our ſtanding Force to ſomething more
than the preſent Eſtabliſhment in time of
peace, theſe two bodies would be a mu-
tual aid and check to each other ; the
laſt would be in the nature of the old feodal Militia, and would more immediately
be under the command of the Crown ;
the firſt would reſemble the old National
Militia, and would in a more eſpecial manner be the Army of the Legiſlature—the
one would repel any ſudden inſult ; the
other any premeditated Invaſion—the one
might on a proper occaſion carry the glory
of our Arms into diſtant Countries ; the
other ſhew the ſtability of them at home ;
—the one would be our offenſive Arms;
the other our defenſive ;—the one would
be the ſword of the Commonwealth ; the
other its impenetrable Buckler ; and both
together would form one uniform plan of
Government, which would make us hardly
ſenſible of the confuſions of war, and re-
duce it almoſt to the calmneſs of peace ;
—the ſame ſteady, manly, regular, conduct would appear in both ; every temporary and violent expedient would be made

un-

unneceffary ; the exorbitance of Taxes would in time be reduced ; and we fhould then no longer be obliged to augment a debt, till at laft it deftroys us,—though perhaps in the midft of fucceffes ; which makes us, in fact, always weaker by our Conquefts, and poorer by our Acquifitions ; and war would then no more be a Fever of the State, which, let the event be good or bad, has conftantly preyed on the vitals of this Country.

Upon the whole, therefore, if it has been fufficiently proved, that in the Plan, which was laft year propofed for eftablifhing a National Militia, the command of it was placed in fuch hands, as the Principles of our Conftitution require,——that the trade of this Country will not be diminifhed at all by fuch an Inftitution ; or if at all, no more than what is abfolutely neceffary for the fecurity of the remainder—that the fcheme itfelf is capable of execution, and will in the event prove adequate to the purpofes for which it was intended ;— that the danger, without it, is imminent, and confequently the neceffity of it apparent ; I flatter myfelf that no farther arguments need be brought in fupport of this Plan.—I hope therefore that every lover of his Country will

concur

concur in promoting it in this Seffion of the *Britifh* Parliament; it cannot perhaps be brought in the firft inftance to perfection; whoever has perufed our Statute Books muft have obferved, that every one of our Inftitutions advanced gradually by various Laws and frequent amendments to their prefent State;— with what zeal will a wife Minifter encourage a fcheme, which will render all his future Toils pleafant and profperous?—And ought not all parties (who equally pretend the good of the whole to be their object) to join in embracing a Defign, on which the fafety of the whole depends—Left therefore we fhould betray our want of that public Spirit, which we all fo loudly profefs, by rejecting the only means of prefervation at this important Crifis, on account of fome neceffary trouble in the execution, and left we fhould thereby expofe thofe facred trufts, in defence of which our Anceftors fought and fell, and which are now configned to our care for the fake of ourfelves and our pofterity.——Let us, like the champion of *Ifrael*, reject the arms of another, for like him we have tried them; they never can properly fit, and their weight may perhaps opprefs us, but with our own ftaves and our

own

own weapons let us deftroy the enemy that defies us.

Other inducements might ftill be urged in fupport of this Plan, if I was inclined to fhew at large the Misfortunes of my Country at a time, when many too much defpair already of its Situation ;—its natives, though by nature brave, are now defpifed and dejected — though wealthy, it is brought into Diftrefs—though powerful, it is become contemptible—its Fleets, though more numerous than at any Period of our Hiftory, are now no longer victorious,—and its wealthy and populous Colonies are every where infulted and invaded by the lefs powerful Settlements of its Enemies ;—a fatal Charm feems to poffefs it, and defeats every advantage which the bountiful Hand of Nature has beftowed upon it.— This melancholy Profpect has made fome Perfons entertain a Sentiment unworthy of a *British* Spirit, that the Power of this Nation is fo far unequal to that of *France*, that we muft fubmit to any Terms of Peace which our Rival fhall impofe upon us.—Shall we, who have voluntarily entered into fo many Wars to fupport the Independency of other Nations, at prefent defpond of our own ?

And

And are we doomed now only to feel ourselves weak, when it is our own Cause in which we are to fight, and our own Country which demands our protection?—The want of Power is not the Cause of our Misfortunes, it is the want only of a proper Method of exerting it;—this Nation has now more than double the strength which it had in the memorable year 1588; and the House of *Austria* was not then less powerful than that of *Bourbon* is at present; we were able, however, at that period, to secure our own Coasts, to annoy those of the Enemy, to defeat his Fleets, and destroy his Settlements in the *Indies*. Let us now, therefore, shew the same wisdom, and exert the same spirit, and we shall extricate ourselves from our present difficulties, not only with safety but with honour. Our first point must be to secure ourselves at home. This effect can alone be produced by the Establishment of a NATIONAL FORCE SUFFICIENT FOR OUR DEFENCE, BUT NO WAYS REPUGNANT TO THE SPIRIT OF OUR CONSTITUTION—a Constitution, which having been preserved (though much in ruins) by Providential Events from the encroaching Spirit of the *Tudors*,—and again rescued by the virtue of our Ancestors from the more hasty violations of the *Stuarts*, has

now

now furvived for almoſt feventy years, repaired, improved, but not wholly perfect; its civil Inſtitutions have been largely and wifely con-fidered,—its Military Eſtabliſhments have been totally neglected; and it has paid moſt dearly for the neglect, by loſſes, by debts, by panics, by diſhonour ;—its cafe is not as yet, however, totally irretrievable ; its may ſtill be able to fubfiſt in its prefent unnatural courfe, until its Inſtitutions have taken effect, provided it haſtens their accompliſhment ; but they will require all our wifdom in the contrivance, and all our vigour in the execution ; and if the Ingratitude of thofe whom we endeavour to ferve, fhould fometimes make our labours unpleafant, we muſt remember, that the End we feek is the Prefervation of our Country. When this Iſland was frequently plundered, and almoſt conquered by the *Danes*, the perfi-dious invaders of ancient times, the caufe of it was, that a proper attention had not been paid to the difcipline of the *Saxon* Militia ; and it is recorded among the wife Inſtitutions of the virtuous *Alfred*, that by new regulations he brought back this once martial body to its firſt ſtate of perfection, and thereby relieved his kingdoms from the fury of *Daniſh* incurfions.—

L   IJE,